Rapping for Shelly

Alles Digitale zu diesem Buch kann auf der Lernplattform
allango von Ernst Klett Sprachen abgerufen werden. So geht's:

| QR-Code scannen oder **www.allango.net** aufrufen | Buchtitel oder ISBN in der Suche eingeben und auf das Buchcover klicken | Zum Inhalt navigieren, direkt abrufen oder speichern |

Dieses Symbol bedeutet, dass zu einem Buch-Abschnitt
ein digitaler Inhalt verfügbar ist.

Paul Davenport

Rapping
for Shelly

Ernst Klett Sprachen
Stuttgart

Hinweis: Das Hörbuch zu Rapping for Shelly (online verfügbar, siehe S. 1 dieses Buches) wurde stellenweise vereinfacht und ist daher nicht durchgehend identisch mit dem gedruckten Text.

1. Auflage 1 [19] [18] [17] [16] [15] | 2028 27 26 25 24

Alle Drucke dieser Auflage sind unverändert und können im Unterricht nebeneinander verwendet werden.
Die letzte Zahl bezeichnet das Jahr des Druckes. Das Werk und seine Teile sind urheberrechtlich geschützt. Jede Nutzung in anderen als den gesetzlich zugelassenen Fällen bedarf der vorherigen schriftlichen Einwilligung des Verlags.

www.klett-sprachen.de

Autor: Dr. Paul Davenport

Redaktion: Paul Newcomb
Layoutkonzeption: Elmar Feuerbach
Gestaltung und Satz: Satzkasten, Stuttgart
Umschlaggestaltung: Elmar Feuerbach
Titelbild: Shutterstock © UltraViolet, New York
Bild vom Autor (S. 6): Photo by Herman Arens
Druck und Bindung: Elanders GmbH, Waiblingen

Printed in Germany
ISBN 978-3-12-542642-9

Contents

*Paul
Davenport*

About the book

16 year-old Sal D'Angelo dreams of becoming a rap superstar. He's got the talent and the determination but he's facing big obstacles. As a Latino, he's definitely an outsider in the mainly Afro-American Frisco rap scene. And the fact that he prefers to rap about life in a middle-class American town rather than the classic theme of life in the ghetto makes him even more of an outsider. Still, with his brilliant style he makes a name for himself, even winning rap battles against some famous rappers. He seems to be on his way to achieving his dream, but then he falls in love with the girlfriend of his biggest rival and worst enemy...

About the author

Music is an important part of several of Paul Davenport's readers. Paul comes from a musical family. One of the happiest memories of his youth is the regular 'jam sessions' with his father, with Paul on alto sax and his father on the piano. (His grandmother actually played background music for silent films!). Paul enjoys a wide range of music styles including pop, rap, country, disco and rock and roll, including songs by German artists.

After completing his postgraduate studies, he moved to Germany, where he's been living with his wife and family ever since.

The roots of his writing career go back to the stage plays he wrote for his English classes to perform. One of them, *The Royal Choice,* became his first publication, in 1996. Four years later, he wrote the first of his many school readers.

A highlight in his writing career was when his story *Crossroads to Love* became a finalist in the Extensive Reading Foundation's contest for reader of the year 2007. The second highlight came a year later, 2008, when another of his stories, *Horror Trip on the Pecos River* was named the winner of that same contest.

Paul's hobbies include reading, table tennis and fly fishing. He sometimes misses the trout fishing in Maine, where he grew up. He still has his alto sax and, from time to time, takes it out and plays a tune or two.

Abbreviations used in annotations:

abb	abbreviation
derog	derogatory
inf	informal
off	offensive
sb	somebody
sl	slang
sth	something
vulg	vulgar

1 THE DREAM

'I'm proud to be Latino,
my father from Mexico,
my mother from Puerto Rico,
born in San Francisco,
5 *I want the world to know*
where my rap is coming from,
where it's gonna go.'

Sal paused and let his words echo in his ear. He
loved the way the words 'rolled', as he liked to say.
10 He loved the sounds of words. He enjoyed putting
them together and watching them interact, the way
they did in the sentences he had just spoken. The
way the words 'Latino', 'Mexico', 'Puerto Rico', 'San
Francisco', 'know' and 'go' all echoed each other. It
15 was like he'd made a necklace with words, linking
the words together, like pearls.

Sal D'Angelo, or Sal D, as he called himself, had
a dream. It was a crazy dream. He wanted – no,
he *yearned* – to become a famous rapper, a rap
20 superstar. He had the talent – a lot of people had
told him that – and he was willing to work hard to
develop it.

But, he realized, there were huge obstacles in
his way. The main one, of course, was the fact that
25 he was a Latino. To most people, the world of rap
music was a black world. They didn't expect to see
a Latino there. Some didn't want to see a Latino
there. If a guy like Sal tried to get in, they would try
to keep him out.

---

1 **Latino** [læˈtiːnoʊ] person who comes from Central America or Puerto Rico (i.e. has
the dark looks of a Spanish/Indian person) – 15 **necklace** [ˈnekləs] a piece of jewelry a
woman wears around her neck – 19 **to yearn** [jɔːn] (for sth): to want sth very much –
23 **obstacle** [ˈɑːbstəkəl] problem, sth is in the way of sth else

Another obstacle was his subject matter. Mainstream rap was about life in the ghetto, a world Sal had no first-hand knowledge of. His world was strictly middle-class: large, comfortable
5 homes complete with two-car garages, in clean and orderly neighborhoods, with little or no crime. He lived near the top of Albany Hill, in the little town of Albany, ten miles from San Francisco, on the opposite side of the bay. On clear days – smog-
10 free days – he could look out his bedroom window and see San Francisco and the Golden Gate Bridge! On very clear days, he could see much more, a breathtaking panorama including Angel Island, Treasure Island, Alcatraz Island and the bridge that
15 made the Golden Gate Bridge look small: Oakland Bay Bridge.

How can you rap about a place with a million-dollar view?

Tough question – but no tougher than the
20 question, how can you rap about a place you know little or nothing about? Sal was facing a rock-and-a-hard-place choice. If he rapped about the ghetto, people would realize that he didn't know what he was talking about and turn away. If he rapped
25 about his middle-class world, people would also turn away. Or would they?

He thought about it long and hard. And the longer and harder he thought about it, the more he realized that what he really wanted to rap about – what he
30 *had* to rap about – was *his* life, not a fantasy life he knew nothing about. He wanted his rap to be real, not fake. That's why the Albany he would rap about wouldn't be the 'Welcome-to-Awesome-Albany'

---

1 **subject matter** the ideas or information contained in a book, film, speech, etc. –
19 **tough** [tʌf] *here:* difficult – 21 **rock-and-a-hard-place** If you find yourself between a
rock and a hard place, you are in a no-win situation – 32 **fake** not genuine, appearing
to be something it is not

for tourists. His rap would be about the dark side of Albany, the side tourists didn't get to see. Where there was just as much struggle as there was in the ghetto, only different.

5   At first glance, it seemed that kids like him from a typical Albany neighborhood had a wonderful life. Sure, they were well taken care of. They lived in nice houses, went to good schools, wore the latest styles. But – and it was a huge but – there was a
10 price for all these privileges. And the price was high – high pressure. Albany was a high-pressure zone. As a kid from Albany, you were under pressure to be an *achiever*. Sure, your parents did a lot for you, supporting your busy self-improvement program
15 (fitness center, weight loss camps, private tutoring, tennis lessons, riding lessons, and all the rest), but they expected a lot in return. They wanted you to be good, or preferably, excellent. To shine – like a star, get high marks in school, go on to the best colleges,
20 and in the end, land a high-paying job.

No wonder a lot of the kids from Albany had alcohol and drug problems.

---

3 **struggle** a hard fight – 9 **style** *here:* fashion – 13 **achiever** someone who is able to reach their goals – 15 **weight loss camp** a type of summer program to help overweight young people lose weight – 15 **private tutoring** being taught by your own personal teacher – 20 **to land** *here:* to get

2 A ROUGH SCENE

Still another obstacle in the way of Sal's dream was the scene, the San Francisco rap scene. It was highly competitive, it was violent, and it was sometimes dangerous. Like the last rap battle Sal took part in.
5 It ended in chaos. The judges had just announced the winner and were handing over the prize money when one of the other rappers came onto the stage, shouted that he was the real winner, grabbed the money and started to run off. Someone stopped
10 him before he got far. But after that, fighting broke out and fists and chairs flew until the police came.

Sal himself was no friend of violence but he was enough of a realist to face the fact that violence was part of the rap scene. He was aware of the danger
15 and it sometimes frightened him, but he knew there was no way around it. Taking part in rap battles was the ladder to success. You had to climb that ladder to get to the top.

To his mother, rap battles were just that – battles.
20 Every time she heard about violence at rap battles she got all upset and started on Sal again. He shouldn't take part in those *awful* contests. He could get *killed*. Why couldn't he do something that wasn't so *dangerous*?
25 Sal felt like walking away when she started talking like that, but he forced himself to stay and listen. It was his way of showing her that he took her fears for him seriously.

---

rough [rʌf] violent – 3 **competitive** [-'---] *here:* a situation in which everyone is trying hard to win – 8 **to grab** to take or hold sb or sth with your hand suddenly, roughly – 17 **ladder to success** a series of stages on the way to achieving success – 21 **to start on** to attack

When he finally got a chance to speak, he told her that he hated violence and kept away from it wherever possible.

These talks always ended the same: with his
5 mother repeating her warnings and Sal promising to be even more careful in the future.

What bothered him even more than violence was losing rap battles he was sure he'd won. Thinking about it, he could get very angry. When he thought
10 about the enthusiastic way the crowd reacted to his performance, and especially the way they sometimes booed the judges' decision when he didn't get first prize, Sal asked himself if the judges were really fair – or did they have their secret
15 favorites?

The only thing he could do about it, he realized, was to become a better rapper. That was the way to win over audiences and in the end, judges, too. He knew that the more the audience was for him, the
20 harder it would be for the judges to be against him.

---

12 **to boo** to show that you don't like a performance by shouting 'boo'

3 RAPPING FOR THE ENGLISH TEACHER

Sal was systematic about improving his rapping skills. He downloaded videos of star rappers, especially his favorites, Spice 1 and Coolio, and studied their styles and their lyrics. And he practiced 5 writing lyrics himself – constantly. He also worked hard at perfecting his beat-boxing technique.

He had a special way of preparing himself for a rap battle. First he'd picture an opponent, someone he knew and didn't like, and then he tried to think 10 of clever ways to diss him. He developed what he called his outside-inside technique. First, he looked for things to criticize on the outside of his opponents: their lifestyle, their looks, the way they dressed, the way they walked, talked, their typical 15 gestures. Then he'd move on to the inside: their personality, their intelligence, their attitudes. His goal was the common goal of all rappers: to find things about his opponents he could focus on and make fun of.

20 What made Sal different from other rappers was the way he went about achieving that goal. Unlike the others, who used massive verbal violence, Sal D was known for his light and humorous style. So humorous that his opponents themselves 25 sometimes had to laugh, too. There was always a smile on his lips, even when delivering his hardest lines. Even in the heat of a rap battle, he stayed cool and always showed respect for his opponent. The crowds loved him for that, and his popularity grew.

4 **lyrics** the words (of the raps) – 6 **beat-boxing** producing musical sounds like drum and bass beats by using your mouth, lips, etc. – 10 **to diss** (inf) to show disrespect for sb – 15 **gesture** ['dʒestʃə·] a movement you make with your hands or your head to express emotion or give information

When he wasn't directly preparing for a rap battle, he was preparing himself indirectly by collecting new ideas. He always carried a notebook around with him and followed the rappers' rule of writing
5 down his good ideas whenever and wherever they came to him.

When Mrs. Hudson, his English teacher, heard that Sal was a talented rapper, she asked him if she could read some of the things he'd written. A
10 week later, she came to him smiling and said she liked his work very much. Would Sal be willing, she asked, to do one of his raps in her English class? Sal hesitated. He didn't feel good about doing a rap at school, in front of his classmates. On the other
15 hand, performing before a live audience was a chance to gain valuable experience. In the end, he said yes.

It was the first class Monday morning when Mrs. Hudson announced that she had a surprise for
20 the class. Sal was going to perform one of his raps. Suddenly all of the sleepy, Monday-morning heads looked up. Monday-morning eyes opened wide in surprise.

Sal got up and went to the front. He grinned at
25 the class. 'This is a rap about a girl I once knew,' he began. From the back of the room came a lovesick voice, 'Ohhhh, Sal,' but the others didn't react. They were looking at Sal expectantly. He started his little ritual, the one he always went through before
30 performing. He closed his eyes and began to nod, listening for the beat in his head. Then he started beat-boxing: boom-wickee-boom, boom-wickee-

13 **to hesitate** to pause because you are uncertain, embarrassed, etc. – 16 **valuable** ['væljuəbl] very useful – 24 **to grin** to smile broadly – 26 **lovesick** very much in love

boom, boom-wickee-boom! Even before he said the first words, the kids were all smiling.

Marie
from Albany
5 *set her heart on*
U of C
at Berkeley.
No big deal,
you say,
10 *but hey!*
She's eating her heart out,
chewing her nails,
tearing her hair,
growing a red, red rash
15 *on her chinny chin, chin,*
waiting for that letter
that says she's in,
hanging onto her hope,
trying to cope
20 *and stay cool*
in her final months
at Albany High School,
but begins to lose it
when one by one,
25 *friends who applied*
got their replies,
came to class
holding them high,
crying, 'I'm in, I'm in!'
30 *And every day*
they ask the same,

---

5 **to set your heart on sth** to want sth very much – 6 **U of C** University of California –
11 **to eat your heart out** to feel sad about sth / sb – 12 **to chew** [tʃuː] **your nails** to keep
biting your fingernails because you are nervous – 14 **rash** an area of red spots on your
skin – 15 **chin** the part of your face below your mouth and above your neck – 19 **to cope**
(with sth) to deal with a problem or task successfully

'You in, Marie,
you in?'
And every day
she has to say
5 *'Nope.*
I haven't heard from them yet.'
What a pain!
She feels so small,
like banging her head on the wall.
10 *Why are they making*
her wait so long?
What's wrong?
Her grades are, uh, okay,
she was in the school play,
15 *she does volunteer work at the zoo,*
she's a cheerleader, too.
Poor Marie!
Using Valium
to get through the day.
20 *Is that any way*
to treat a girl
who's so ambitious,
whose only wish is
to go to college?
25 *There must be some mistake.*
Did her letter get lost,
was it misplaced?
If they only knew
what she's going through.
30 *She's lost so much weight.*
Please U of C,
send that letter today,

---

9 **to bang** to hit – 13 **grade** a mark given for an examination or a piece of school work –
15 **volunteer work** unpaid work – 21 **to treat** to behave in a particular way toward sb

before it's too late!
The letter comes finally,
words like a snake
twist round her neck,
5   *'We regret to inform you..,'*
she can't breathe,
falls to her knees,
her dream falling
round her,
10   *passes out on the floor,*
can't take no more.
Poor Marie!
The doctors agree
it's best
15   *she take a long rest.*

The kids applauded enthusiastically. Sal knew, of course, that some of their enthusiasm had to do with the fact that he had helped shorten what was for many a very long lesson. Mrs. Hudson wasn't the
20   most interesting teacher at Albany Middle School. Still, Sal was pleased.

---

5 **to regret** [rɪˈgret] to feel sorry about sth you've done or haven't done – 10 **to pass out** to fall into a sleep-like state

4   ALONZO'S ANGER

As word went around the school that Sal had done a cool rap in his English class, he was asked to perform it in other classes, too. As the weeks went by, this happened more and more often. So often
5 that the principal had to put a stop to it. Sal was missing too many classes, he said.

By that time Sal had become the talk of the school. So it was only a matter of time until Alonzo Russell aka Big Zo heard about him.

10 Alonzo was sitting at his regular table at the back of the cafeteria. Beside him was his girlfriend, Shelly Carroll. As usual, he was scanning the room, checking to see if he was getting the necessary amount of attention – the amount of attention he
15 felt he deserved as an up and coming rap superstar. At 16, Alonzo was already well known at Albany High and had even begun to make a name for himself in the San Francisco rap scene.

He needn't have looked around. He was getting
20 lots of attention. He always did. Not only at school but everywhere he went. Even those who knew nothing about him as a rapper turned their heads to get a glimpse of the tall, good-looking young Afro-American wearing the latest ghetto look.

25 Shelly was watching him, trying to decide what to do. She wanted to tell him about Sal, but she was afraid he wouldn't like what she had to say. In the end, her need to tell him the news was stronger than her fear. She waited until he started eating,

---

5 **to put a stop to sth** to stop sth – 9 **aka** [ˌeɪˌkeɪˈeɪ] *(abb) short for*: also known as –
15 **up and coming... superstar** Soon he will be a superstar. – 23 **glimpse** [glɪmps] look, view

then said, 'Have you heard about the kid who's been rapping here at school?'

'Huh? What kid?' Alonzo stopped chewing on his hamburger and stared at her. 'What you talking about, girl?'

'A kid – you know him – Sal D'Angelo – has been rapping here in school.'

'Sal D? Rapping in school? Where' that at?'

'It started with his English teacher. He did a rap in her class and then – it was like a chain reaction! – they kept asking him to rap in other classes. The kids loved it. He's like, very talented, they say.'

There was a sudden flash of anger in Alonzo's eyes. 'What was that? What you just say, girl?' he almost shouted.

Shelly lowered her voice. 'Uh, Sal D'Angelo. He's, uh, very talented, they say.'

Alonzo speared a French fry and sucked it slowly into his mouth. 'Well, they dead wrong about that! There's only one talented rapper in this school and his name ain't D'Angelo! It's me, Big Zo, Alonzo Russell! Got that? The next time you see him, tell him the rap scene is a black scene, ain't for no dumb Spics like him. Tell him that's a personal message from Big Zo.'

Just then someone Alonzo knew stopped at his table. 'Hey, man. Have you heard about Sal D'Angelo?'

'Get lost!' Alonzo said with a wave of his hand.

Alonzo went back to his food. For the next few minutes all he did was eat. Finally, when he was

---

4 **What you...?** (sl) What are you...? – 8 **Where' that at?** (sl) "What do you mean?" / "What's all this about?" – 10 **chain reaction** a series of events, each of which causes the next – 13 **flash** here: sudden sign or expression – 18 **to spear** [spɪr] here: to push the fork into – 23 **ain't** (sl) isn't – 24 **dumb** [dʌm] (sl) stupid – 24 **Spic** [spɪk] (derog) a very offensive word for Latin Americans. According to one theory, the word comes from the way Spanish-speaking people say 'speak'. – 24 **dat** (sl) that – 29 **wave** moving your hand from side to side

finished, he looked up at Shelly. 'You gone see this dude rap you'self?'

'Yeah. Yesterday. In my history class.'

'Well?' Alonzo's eyes were burning into Shelly's.

5 'Uh, some of the kids were like, enthusiastic. He *was* good, but, uh, not all that good.'

Alonzo gave Shelly a little grin. It was an I-forgive-you-for-saying-something-stupid grin. He shook his head slowly.

10 After a few moments, Shelly got nervous. 'Hey, I only said he was good. I didn't say he was as good as you, did I? You're in another league, a class all by yourself. He can't touch you, Zo.'

Alonzo stared at her but said nothing.

15 'Zo? Aw, come on. I take it all back, okay? Compared with you, he's definitely second class.' Shelly tried to smile but it came out twisted. She let out a nervous little laugh and put her hand on his.

Alonzo's cool grin appeared again. 'So tell me 20 about the rap. What was the dude rapping about?'

'About a girl who had a nervous breakdown when she was turned down by the college she wanted to go to.'

Alonzo's mouth fell open. His eyes grew cold. 25 'That's not right. That ain't something you rap about!'

Confused, Shelly gave him a disbelieving look. 'What do you mean? It was very serious – and realistic. It happens all the time. I know kids like 30 her.'

Alonzo shook his head. 'You gotta be kiddin'! I know kids like that, too. She probably thought she

---

1 **You gone see...?** *(sl)* Did you go and see...? – 17 **twisted** not normal, strange in an unpleasant way – 21 **nervous breakdown** a mental illness in which sb becomes very depressed – 31 **you gotta be kiddin'** (you've got to be kidding) said to show that you are very surprised at sth that has just been said

could get into college just because her old man is president of the bank or something like that. But that ain't the point. The point is, you don't rap about no middle-class shit like that. Rap is ghetto music,
5 about real problems.'

Shelly shook her head. 'Come on, Zo. That's not fair!'

'Don't give me that 'not fair' crap! Compared with the problems the brothers and sisters face, not
10 getting accepted by a college is a joke, man!'

Shelly stared at him, her eyes full of the question: do you really mean this?

Alonzo stared back a moment, then broke out in wild laughter, causing several heads to turn his
15 way. When he finished laughing, he nodded his head, suddenly serious again. 'Wait till the brothers hear about this,' he said. 'Sal D will be finished in the rap scene. A rap about some spoiled bitch getting turned down by a college? Ha! He won't
20 get no respect no more. Anyone who raps about something like that don't know what rap is about, man!'

Shelly only nodded. She knew better than to say too much when Alonzo was angry.

25 'That's the end of Sal D – but just to make sure I'm gonna spread the word so the right people hear about this!'

He grinned at Shelly. She nodded again. She could see that he was very pleased with himself.
30 She didn't want to, but when he kept grinning at her, she finally had to grin back.

---

8 **crap** *(vulg)* nonsense – 9 **brothers and sisters** *(dialect)* friends (black) – 18 **spoiled** [spɔɪld] *(AE; BE: spoilt)* A spoiled person is one whose character has turned out badly because they were given everything they wanted as children. – 18 **bitch** a potentially offensive word for a woman – 19 **won't get no** In colloquial language, people often use "double negatives", but the meaning is still positive, e.g. "He won't get no respect." means "He won't get any respect."

5 CONFRONTATION

In the following days, Alonzo did just that – he spread the word about Sal. Then, about a week after his conversation with Shelly, he was in the audience at Minna's, San Francisco's hot spot for
5 rappers, waiting for the weekly rap battle to begin. Shelly was at his side. In a couple of minutes, he knew, it would be Sal D's turn to take the stage. Alonzo looked around. The brothers were all there. They were all looking at him, waiting for his signal.

10 A moment later, the DJ announced Sal and his opponent. As soon as the two of them came onto the stage, Alonzo gave the signal and Sal was greeted by a wave of boos and shouts. Then he started a chant, 'Go home, Sal D!', and the others
15 joined in. Taken by surprise, Sal stood very still and scanned the sea of faces. If Alonzo had thought that he would be frightened, he was wrong about that. Sal was looking for him and soon found him. Immediately, Sal's eyes locked onto his. Alonzo
20 stopped shouting. He couldn't go on. There was something about the boy's look that was getting into his head.

When the others saw that Alonzo had stopped shouting, they stopped, too. The DJ noticed this
25 and told the two rappers to get started. Sal went first and gave a brilliant performance, full of his typical humor. His opponent did his best to outdo him, but his attacks were over the top and fell flat.

---

2 **to spread the word** to talk about (to many people) – 4 **hot spot** favorite, popular place – 14 **chant** [tʃænt] words that a group of people shout or sing again and again – 19 **to lock onto** to fix onto – 27 **to outdo** [aʊt'duː] If you outdo sb, you do sth better than they do – 28 **over the top** unacceptable because it is too extreme

The next day at school Sal sat in a corner of the cafeteria, watching Alonzo, waiting for a chance to talk to him. As usual, he was surrounded by friends, including his girlfriend, Shelly Carroll. Sal waited
5 until only Shelly was left, then went over to Alonzo's table and sat down. Immediately, Alonzo got up to go. 'Come on, Shelly,' he said.

'Wait a minute. I want to talk to you,' Sal said.

'I don't wanna talk to you.'

10 'Are you sure about that?'

'Huh?' Alonzo hesitated. 'Why should I talk to you?'

'We're both rappers,' Sal said. 'We've got a lot in common.'

15 'Ha! That's a good joke,' Alonzo said. He looked at his watch. 'You got five minutes, man.' He turned to Shelly and said, 'Go ahead, baby. Wait for me outside. This won't take long.'

As Shelly turned to go, Sal's heart did a jump
20 when he noticed a little smile on her face – for him!

Alonzo sat down and gave Sal a bored look. 'So. What's on your mind, man?'

'I saw you Saturday night at Minna's,' Sal said.

'So what?'

25 'You were shouting at me.'

'Could be.'

Sal leaned forward and looked Alonzo in the eye. 'I heard you didn't like the rap I did at school. What was wrong with it?'

30 'Wrong? It was more than wrong, it was gross! Listen, dude,' Alonzo said, poking his finger at Sal, 'rap is like, serious. You don't use rap to talk about some spoiled chick who lost her college!'

---

30 **gross** [grəʊs] *here:* totally wrong – 31 **dude** [duːd] *(inf)* an informal term of address similar to 'man' – 31 **to poke** to push quickly – 33 **chick** *(inf)* a girl or woman

'Hey, my English teacher wanted me to do it, okay?'

'Don't play dumb with me, D'Angelo. I'm talkin' about *what* you rapped about, not *who* you did it for. You know that!'

Sal thought fast. He didn't want Alonzo to be his enemy but, at the same time, he had to stand up for his position on rap. Sal tried to look Alonzo in the eye but Alonzo took out his cell phone and began to play with it, flipping it open and shut. Sal watched him a while. When he finally stopped, Sal fixed his eyes on his and said, 'I don't get it. What's the name of the game you're playing?'

'Game? What game?' Alonzo gave him a flat look.

'You're just as middle-class as I am and you know it! I've been in your part of town. I know where you live.'

Caught by surprise, Alonzo sat back, his eyes huge. 'So what? What's that got to do with anything?'

'What's all this stuff about the ghetto? What do you know about the ghetto? There's no ghetto here in Albany.'

Alonzo had regained his cool. There was a little grin on his face now. 'This ain't about me, man. It's about rap, about the rap tradition. I respect that tradition, man. I don't go screwing around with it like you!'

'You mean – '

'Yeah, I mean that rap is all about the ghetto. Rap *is* ghetto. That's the rap tradition, you hear? You don't screw with tradition!'

'Tradition? That's a big word! Rap is what, twenty-five years old? Thirty, tops. And it's been growing

---

3 **to play dumb** act as if you don't know anything – 26 **to screw around with sth** to use sth in a careless way – 33 **tops** *(sl)* at the most

and changing since the beginning. Guys rap all over the world.' Sal shook his head. 'How can you say it's got to be like this or like that?'

Alonzo looked at his watch and grinned. 'Your five minutes are up, dude.'

'You talk about respect. How about a little respect for me and my kind of rap?'

'You're out of bounds, D'Angelo. You put yourself there. It's your problem, not mine.'

Sal's eyes searched his face. 'But I – '

'Forget it, man.' Alonzo got up and turned to go.

'Alonzo?'

'Yeah?'

'Here's something for you to think about before you go: It's very possible we'll meet in a rap battle one of these days...'

Alonzo gave him a twisted grin. 'That's gonna be a black day for you, dude! Get it? A BLACK DAY!'

He let out a wild laugh, turned and walked away.

8 **out of bounds** [baʊndz] outside of where you're allowed to be

6   BODYGUARDS

Sal thought about his talk with Alonzo for days. He couldn't get it out of his head. Especially the angry way it ended. He had the feeling something bad was going to happen.

5   So what took place a few weeks later came as no surprise to him. It was a Saturday night at Minna's. A few minutes before it was Sal's turn to go on stage a group of boys came up to him and pushed him into a dark corner. They were wearing masks.

10   One of them said, 'This no place for a greasy Spic!' Another said, 'Spics ain't welcome here!' and hit him on the head.

Before Sal could cry out, one of the boys grabbed his arms and held them behind his back. Then

15   another hit him in the stomach. Sal fell to the floor. They began to kick him. Instinctively, Sal rolled himself up into a ball with his arms around his head. Just before he passed out he heard a voice say, 'Leave him alone!'

20   Later, in the hospital, the doctor said he was lucky that they hadn't kicked him in the head. He had several bruises but only one serious injury: a broken rib.

His mother's reaction didn't surprise him. Now

25   that her worst fears had come true, she said she hoped he had learned his lesson and would stay away from the rap scene in the future. Sal, still in the hospital, said he would think seriously about it.

It didn't take him long to figure out what he had

30   to do. He had to get himself a bodyguard or two.

---

10 **greasy** ['griːsi] (of hair or skin) producing too much oil – 15 **stomach** ['stʌmək] the front part of the body below the heart – 22 **bruise** [bruːz] a blue, brown or purple mark on the skin that you get after you fall or are hit – 23 **rib** any of the curved bones that surround the chest – 29 **to figure** ['fɪɡjʊr] **out** to understand better

Immediately, he thought of Marty and George Hawkins, both of them big, strong boys, both on the school's wrestling team. And, best of all, both big fans of Sal D's. They had even sent him a text
5 message saying get well soon.

When he asked if they would be his bodyguards, they said yes immediately. In fact, Marty said that since hearing about his beating they had been intending to ask him that very same question.

10 Sal's mother wasn't pleased when Sal told her he was going to go on taking part in rap battles, but the idea that he would have bodyguards did make her feel better about it. Especially after she met Marty and George, the 'giants', as she called them. Sal had
15 asked them to drop by for exactly that reason – to make her feel better.

14 **giant** ['dʒaɪənt] a very large, strong person – 15 **to drop by** to visit

7   UNDER CONTRACT

Marty and George were good bodyguards. They accompanied Sal to the rap battles and kept a close eye on him. He felt safe and was able to concentrate fully on his performance. That was good for Sal, but
5 bad for his opponents.

He won rap battles regularly now, even beating some of the big names in the area, like Penny Wise or Reverend Jake. Slowly but surely, he was making
10 a name for himself in the San Francisco rap scene. In fact, a talent scout for Stan Silverton, the well-known music agent, had heard about him and came to see him perform. Afterwards, he told Sal that Mr. Silverton would like to meet him. Sal couldn't believe his good luck.

15 As the day of the meeting came nearer, Sal grew more and more excited. A lot depended on the meeting. He realized what a man like Mr. Silverton could do for his career. With his connections, he could open a lot of doors for Sal, doors that Sal
20 didn't even know about. Wanting to make a good impression on the man, Sal did some Internet research on him. He was especially interested in what those who worked with him had to say. 'Hard but fair' was the main opinion. By 'hard' was meant
25 that Mr. Silverton expected those he had under contract to do what the contract said. When word got back to him, for example, that one of his artists didn't show up for a performance or even showed up too late, they got only one warning. The second
30 time it happened, the contract was canceled. That

---

10 **talent scout** person who tries to find talented people that he can then make famous – 18 **connections** people you know – 28 **to show up** to arrive

was fine with Sal, who had a very professional attitude about his rap career anyway.

When he arrived at the agent's office several minutes before his appointment, Mr. Silverton's
5 secretary flashed him a smile and asked him to take a seat. Sal sat down and looked around. The walls were covered with photos of stars and other famous people together with Mr. Silverton. Sal's eyes grew huge as they jumped from photo to photo. Oh,
10 man! Justin Timberlake, Pink, Rianna and – hey! – there was even Dr. Dre and Ice Cube!

Suddenly, the man from the photos was standing in front of him, holding out his hand. 'Hi,' he said. 'I'm Stan Silverton. Glad to meet you!' Sal shot up
15 from his seat and pumped Mr. Silverton's hand. 'Come on into my office,' he said and opened the door for Sal. It was a large office. The walls were filled with more photos of famous people. Mr. Silverton sat down behind his desk and motioned
20 for Sal to sit opposite him.

Mr. Silverton gave Sal a warm, fatherly smile. 'My man Ricky tells me you're good. He's one of my best scouts. When he says someone is good, they *are* good.'
25 Sal felt his face grow warm. 'Thank you, Mr. Silverton.'

'Ricky says you're still in school. Is that right?'

Sal nodded. 'That's right, sir.'

'You want to finish school, I assume.'
30 Again, Sal nodded.

'Well, that's a good idea. The music business is risky. It's important to have something to fall back

---

19 **to motion** ['mouʃən] to make a movement with your hand to show sb what they should do – 32 **to fall back on** to have sth to use when you are in difficulty

on.' Mr. Silverton sat back in his chair and smiled at Sal.

Sal smiled back.

'So we'll start you out slow and easy. One gig a week. Saturday nights. At the Hard Rock Café, with DJ Thomson.'

Sal's eyes went wide. He drew in a deep breath. 'At the Hard Rock Café? Oh, man!'

'Does that mean you agree?' Mr. Silverton laughed softly.

Sal nodded and laughed. 'Yes, sir!'

After some friendly small talk, Mr. Silverton got out a contract and began to explain it. Sal listened carefully and asked a few questions. In the end, Mr. Silverton stood up and came around his desk. 'You've got great potential, Sal. I want you to realize that potential. If you follow the rules and do what's in the contract, you'll be on your way. It's an important first step for you.'

Smiling, he put his hand on Sal's shoulder. Sal stood up. 'Welcome to the Silverton family,' Mr. Silverton said, shaking his hand. 'You're not of age yet, but that's no problem. You just have to get your parents to sign the contract.'

Sal nodded, thinking: that's not going to be easy.

That evening he sat down with his mother to discuss the contract with her. He began by describing Mr. Silverton's office and the photos he'd seen of all the famous people together with Mr. Silverton. He noticed how her eyes lighted up when he mentioned some of the older stars in the photos like Barry Manilow, Phil Collins or Neil Diamond, so he went on naming all the older ones he could

---

4 **gig** a performance – 22 **of age** old enough to be legally independent, e.g. to vote in an election

remember. Before talking about the meeting itself, he emphasized what Mr. Silverton had said about school: that he wanted the boy to start slowly and not do too much while he was still in school, and that it was important for him to finish school. His mother nodded. A smile crossed her face. So far, so good, thought Sal.

But in the end, when it was time for her to sign the contract, she suddenly grew nervous and asked him if he was sure he was making the right decision. He said yes, he was, and she repeated the question: was he sure he could do all that, and keep up with his schoolwork? He was sure, he said. Very sure? Very sure. Finally, she signed the contract.

8 AN UNUSUAL CONVERSATION

Sal was wired with excitement. He had no sooner sent off the signed contract to Mr. Silverton than he began to think about his debut at the Hard Rock Café. He already had a sizeable collection of his
5 own songs, more than enough for a gig like that, but he wanted to write something new for this special occasion. He wanted to get off to a good start, and give the customers at the café the best music he could write. His first performance was
10 only a month and a half away, so he would have to work quickly. He already knew what he would write about: life in his hometown of Albany. That was Sal D's theme. He wasn't going to change it for Alonzo or anyone else!
15 And so began a creative phase, an exciting time in which Sal's head buzzed with ideas. He spent most of his free time in the cellar with his keyboard, testing new beats and lyrics. It was a happy time for Sal.
20 It wasn't such a happy time for his mother and friends. It was like he had gone off to another world and left them behind. His head full of music, Sal's ability to carry on a conversation was very limited. He smiled and said 'yeah' or 'right' a lot. He had a
25 faraway look in his eye.
Some of his friends considered that funny, but his mother wasn't amused. She missed his humor, his day-to-day commentary on the world around him, their interesting conversations. And she was
30 worried about his schoolwork. When she asked him

---

1 **wired** ['waɪərd] very nervous, excited – 4 **sizeable** ['saɪzəbl] quite large – 16 **to buzz** [bʌz] **with** to be full of excitement and activity

about it (every day), all she got was a smile and a mumble.

As weeks went by and Sal spent even more time in the cellar, her worries grew. At last, she decided that the time had come to have a serious talk with him.

She waited for the right moment. It came a few days later, when he returned home from school. She was in the kitchen making coffee, waiting for him, knowing that it was always the first place he went before disappearing in the cellar.

'Hi, Sal,' she said as he came in. 'How was school today?'

'Okay, I guess,' he said as he headed for the refrigerator.

'Any highlights you want to tell me about?' she said with a twisted grin.

'Highlights?' Sal paused as he made himself a glass of chocolate milk. 'No. No highlights but lots of low lights!' He laughed nervously.

'Tell me about them. Could it be that they have something to do with not paying attention in class or not doing your homework?'

'Aw come on, Mom. Don't start on that again!' Sal got very busy drinking his milk.

She poured herself a cup of coffee and watched him a moment in silence. When it became obvious that he wasn't going to answer her question, she went straight to the point. 'Do you think you're doing the right thing, spending all your free time on your music? Do you realize what it's doing to you?'

When he looked at her as if he didn't know what she was talking about, she explained how his work

---

2 **mumble** ['mʌmbəl] words spoken so quietly that they are not clear – 29 **to go straight to the point** to say sth in a direct way without extra information or feelings

on his songs was changing him. How the focal point of his life had moved away from school, friends and home to the cellar, to his keyboard and his music. She could understand, she said, that his first big gig was important to him and that he wanted to make a good first impression with some fresh, new songs. 'But,' she said firmly, 'aren't you taking it a little too far? Across the line?'

'Line?'

'I'm talking about the line between your everyday life, school, friends and home on the one side and your music on the other.' She paused, fixing her eyes on his. 'I don't very often give you advice but – shouldn't you try to keep a balance between the two?' She paused again, choosing her words carefully. 'I'm not good at warnings, but I see a danger here – that you're letting your music take over your life. That's not good for your life and it probably isn't good for your music, either.'

Sal glanced at her. He saw the serious look in her eyes. After a while, he nodded.

'I see what you mean,' he said slowly.

A warm smile crossed his mother's face. 'I hoped you would,' she said. 'Sorry if I went over the top. I'm just trying to help. You know that.'

Sal took a last long drink of his chocolate milk. 'You didn't go over the top,' he said with a little smile.

His mother looked at him a moment, then smiled back.

'Is it alright if I pinch you once in a while?'

Surprised by his mother's sudden playful look, Sal shook his head. 'Pinch me?'

6 **to make a good first impression** to have a strong, positive effect on people – 31 **to pinch** [pɪnʃ] to take a piece of someone's skin in your fingers and press it together

'Right. If I notice that you seem to be dreaming about your music when you should be doing something else, like having a conversation with me or doing your homework, I'll give you a little pinch
5 to wake you up.'

Sal laughed. 'That's fine with me – but not too hard!'

'Just hard enough to get you back to earth. You know, that place where the rest of us live.'

10 Sal laughed. '*Now* you're going over the top. But okay – I get your point.' Sal finished his milk and got up to go.

'Uh, Sal. While we're having a little talk, there's something else I wanted to ask you about,' she said,
15 a sly look in her eye.

'Yeah?'

'Girls.'

'Girls? What about them?'

'Come on, Sal. A good-looking boy like you, and
20 so well known, too – because of your music – I'll bet the girls are standing in line just to get a look at you.'

'Well, I have noticed that they've begun to notice me,' he said in a mock serious voice.

25 His mother laughed. 'And?'

Sal hesitated a long moment, then sat down again. 'Do you really want to know?'

'Of course. I'm your mother, aren't I?'

Sal gave her a little smile. 'It's not any of those
30 – the ones in line. It's another girl, one that's not standing in line.'

---

15 **sly** [slaɪ] as if you know a secret (but do not tell anyone this) – 24 **mock serious** pretending to be serious

His mother gave him a knowing smile and nodded. 'Right. That's the kind guys often find the most interesting. I was one of those myself.'

Sal's mouth fell open. 'You were?'

5 She took a short drink of her coffee and looked at him. 'When I first saw your father I thought, Wow! That's the man for me! But I wasn't the only one. Several other girls thought the same thing and really went after him. It wasn't easy to stand by and watch
10 them throw themselves at him, but I hung back and waited for my chance. And you know what?'

'What?'

'It was the right thing to do. After a while, he began to notice me.' She paused, nodding her head
15 thoughtfully. 'It's better that way.'

Sal said nothing. He was looking at his mother with wide-open eyes. He had never had a conversation like this with her before.

---

10 **to hang back** to remain behind

9   TESTING SHELLY

Sal had been open with his mother, but not completely. He had told her about the girl he had his eye on. What he hadn't told her about was the fact that she already had a boyfriend and – that
5 boyfriend was his number one enemy! It was better that his mother didn't know about that.

Thinking about what his mother had said about herself, he began to wonder about Shelly. Was she 'hanging back' the way his mom had done with
10 his dad, or was she just not interested in him? Or – there was a third possibility he had been thinking a lot about lately – did she like him but was too afraid of Alonzo to show it? Sometimes she took quick, secret looks at him. Was it because she was afraid
15 Alonzo might notice something? What were her true feelings about him?

He decided that he would find out. He was going to test her.

He got his chance the next day during his Phys
20 Ed lesson. Mr. Hurley had taken Sal's class out for a run in the woods behind the school. The problem was, Shelly was a slow runner, always at the end of the line and Sal was a strong runner, usually right up front. Sal decided that the best way to get to talk
25 to her would be to fake an injury.

The class, with Mr. Hurley in the lead, had just entered the woods when Sal started limping. He didn't stop running at once. He just limped along as the others ran by him. Finally, when only Shelly was
30 still behind him, he stopped and held onto his leg.

---

19 **Phys Ed** short for 'physical education', sport and exercise taught in schools – 25 **to fake an injury** to act as if he had an injury – 27 **to limp** to walk with difficulty or unevenly because one of your legs is hurt

When Shelly reached him, she hesitated, then ran on by. Sal wanted badly to cry out to her, but somehow kept the cry inside. A moment later, she stopped and turned around. She looked at him for several seconds, then started walking slowly back towards him. Sal could hardly keep from grinning. 'What's wrong?' she said as she got closer. There was a worried look on her face.

'It's my knee. It's a, uh, an old injury from breakdancing.'

'Hey! I didn't know you were into breakdancing.' Shelly's eyes lighted up.

'I – uh, I'm not anymore. I gave it up a few years back.' Sal let out a nervous laugh.

'Do you need any help?'

'Oh, no. I – I can get back on my own.' Sal took a little step as if his leg was in great pain. He gave her his best feel-sorry-for-me smile and said, 'I'll be alright. You go on ahead.'

Again Shelly hesitated. 'Are – you sure?'

'I'll get back somehow.' He put a lot of pain in the word 'somehow.'

'I'd like to help you – I really would but – 'she looked around nervously, 'but if Alonzo heard that I was talking to you, I'd be in deep trouble.'

Sal nodded. 'Hey, I don't want to get you in any trouble. You'd better go now. Don't worry about me. I'll be okay.'

But of course he was thinking: please stay.

Suddenly, Shelly reached out and touched Sal's arm. His heart did a flip. He looked her in the eye. Shelly looked back at him for a moment, hesitated, then turned quickly and started running. Sal's heart

11 **to be into** to like, **to be into sth** to like sth

seemed to stop beating as he watched her go. Just before she was out of sight, she stopped and turned around. Sal waved to her. Shelly looked at him a moment, then waved back. A warm happy feeling
5 ran all through Sal's body.

10 ALICIA'S PARTY

Of course, Sal had been at the top of the invitation list. After all, the party was being given by one of those girls who was standing in line for Sal, as his mother put it. And he had come – but not alone. Since his talk with Shelly, Sal was being very careful. Wherever he went, he took Marty or George along, or sometimes both of them.

Tonight George was with him.

Alicia Pitt was almost a neighbor of his. She lived on Albany Hill, too, only a couple of streets down. Tonight the house was hers. Her parents were spending the weekend in the mountains, hiking. They had always taken Alicia with them but she had reached the age where parties were more interesting than hiking. Most interesting of all at the moment was a boy named Sal. She hoped that she and Sal could get to know each other better at her party. In fact, that was the reason she had arranged it in the first place.

When Sal arrived with George, Alicia came to the door, all smiles. She seemed a little disappointed when she caught sight of the boy beside him but tried not to show it. She took Sal by the hand and steered him through the crowded living room to the kitchen, where she offered the two of them something to drink. She wanted to talk with Sal but felt uncomfortable with George towering beside him. She excused herself, saying that she had to attend to the others, thinking that she'd get back to Sal when George wasn't around.

---

24 **to steer** [stɪr] When you steer a car, boat, etc., you control it so it goes where you want it to go. – 27 **to tower (over)** Sb who towers over others is a lot taller than they are. – 29 **to attend to sb** to look after sb (e.g. here: get them a drink, check they have sb to talk to, etc)

Left to themselves, Sal and George wandered into the living room. The loud music made it almost impossible to talk, so they stood near a wall and looked around. Suddenly – there – on the other side
5 of the room – Sal caught sight of Alonzo with Shelly! Shelly's eyes were on him. Be careful, they seemed to be saying. For a moment, Sal thought about slipping away. Maybe it was the best thing to do. But then he realized that if Alonzo saw him leave or
10 heard that he had been at the party and left early, he might think that Sal was afraid of him. And Sal didn't want him to have that impression.

So he stayed where he was, with George at his side. He tried to talk with George but the music was
15 too loud and he gave up. After a while, Alicia came over to him and asked him if he would dance with her. After they had danced a few minutes, Alicia took him into the kitchen. She wanted to talk to him – alone, she said.
20 She said she had watched him perform at rap battles several times and was one of his biggest fans. She had heard that he now had an agent, she said, and that he would soon have his debut at the Hard Rock Café. Was he excited about it? She had
25 also heard that he was busy writing new songs for his opening night (how did she know all these things?) and wondered how many he had written so far. She gave him a sad look and said she hadn't seen much of him lately. Where had he been? Was
30 he working full-time on the songs?

When she'd finished asking what seemed to Sal like a hundred questions, she gave him a sly smile and said that she had planned something special

8 **to slip away** to move away quietly without being noticed

for the evening. Would he be willing to take part in a little rap battle? It would be the hit of the party, she said.

Sal was about to ask who the opponent was when it came to him. 'Against Alonzo. Right?'

Alicia let out a little laugh. 'Right! What do you say?'

'I say,' Sal hesitated for effect, 'bring him on!'

'Oh, Sal. I knew you'd say yes!' she said breathlessly, throwing herself in his arms. 'I'll get everything ready.' She gave him a quick kiss on the cheek and hurried out.

At that moment, George came into the kitchen looking for him. 'Hey, what's up? What are you grinning about?'

'Alicia has organized a rap battle.'

'What's so funny about that?'

'Between Big Zo and me.'

'He's got some friends with him.'

'I've got one, too,' Sal said with a playful smile.

5 **to come to** to enter your mind

11 RAP BATTLE

A few minutes later, Alicia turned off the music, got up on a chair and in a loud voice asked the crowd to be quiet a moment. 'As some of you know, we're going to have a rap battle here tonight,' she said,
5 'between two guys we all know, two guys who are already pretty famous in the Frisco rap scene.'

Alicia paused as the kids looked around, trying to catch sight of the two boys. 'I'm talking about Big Zo and Sal D!' Immediately, the room filled with
10 loud cries and applause as the two of them made their way through the crowd to where Alicia was standing. When they had quieted down again, Alicia showed the two boys a coin, then flipped it. Sal won the toss and said he wanted to go second. 'Okay,'
15 she said. 'Each of you has one minute. Make the most of it and may the best man win! The winner will be decided by the amount of applause.'

Alonzo started off. As usual, he was very aggressive, looking Sal up and down and then
20 comparing him to a boxer in the featherweight division, hopelessly outclassed by a heavyweight like himself. His last lines were:

'What I say?
He's a featherweight,
25 *a feather in the wind.*
I'm the wind,
I'm gonna blow him away!'

---

6 **Frisco** *(abb, sl)* San Francisco – 14 **to win the toss** to guess correctly which side of a coin faces upwards when it lands after being thrown in the air – 20 **featherweight** ['feðəˌweɪt] a small, light boxer, weighing between 53 and 57 kilograms – 21 **outclassed** [ˌaʊt'klæst] not as good as sb else at a particular activity – 27 **to blow away** to defeat or even kill

When he finished, he stepped up very close to Sal and blew into his face. A loud 'Ohhhh' came from the crowd. They watched, wide-eyed, to see how Sal would react.

5 All he did was look Alonzo in the eye and shake his head.

Then it was his turn. First came the ritual he always began with. For several seconds he stood very still with his eyes closed. Then he moved his
10 head slowly, from side to side, getting the beat. Then he started beat-boxing. Boom-wickee-boom, boom-wickee-boom. Finally, he opened his eyes and started rapping, slowly at first but quickly gaining speed.

15 *'Big Zo is a hot shot*
wearin' tight jeans,
walkin' like a peacock,
talkin' like he walks
in his Reebocks,
20 *sayin'*
I'm hot, man,
the hottest in the school, man.
Dresses in brand names,
Timberlands and
25 *Air Jordans,*
Phat Fashions,
his hoody a goodie
by Gino,
no no-names,
30 *no hand-me-downs,*
only brand names.
for Big Zo.

17 **peacock** ['piːkɑːk] a large, very beautiful bird – 27 **hoody** ['hʊdi] a sweatshirt with a part you can pull up over your head

He's branded.
That's the name of his game!
Underneath those fancy clothes
there's a heart of gold,
5 *pure gold,*
shining like the sun,
like his rings and things.
Searchin' for
a heart of gold?
10 *He's got it,*
a heart for rich and poor,
young and old,
he's known
for his generosity.
15 *His heart of gold*
knows no boundaries.
He gives till it hurts,
but he got a low
pain threshold,
20 *so low*
he holds onto his gold.
Poor little Big Zo!'

A roar of laughter came from the crowd. Sal waited
a moment before going on to his final lines.

25 *'Gold on the outside,*
gold on the inside,
Big Zo's a gold mine,
gold in his soul,
so deep down,
30 *deep, deep down*
it's never been found!'

---

14 **generosity** kindness, doing or giving more than is expected – 18 **low pain threshold**
unable to bear much pain – 23 **roar** [rɔːr] a loud deep sound

It was obvious who had won. The applause for Sal's performance was long and loud – clearly longer and louder than for Alonzo's. He was standing in a corner with his friends, his face growing darker by the minute.

When the applause finally died down, he went over to Sal, got up close to him, and blew in his face again! Again a loud 'Ohhhh!' went through the crowd. Everyone stepped back, watching, pop-eyed, as Alonzo moved his face closer and closer to Sal's until their noses were almost touching. Everyone thought that Sal would try to push him away, but Sal didn't move. The only change in him was – a little smile came across his face. Alonzo freaked out when he saw that and pushed Sal against the wall. He was about to hit him when George grabbed him from behind and spun him around.

'Hey, be cool, man!' Alonzo said, smiling at the big boy.

'You be cool, too, dude,' George said.

'I think you'd better leave!' Alicia said to Alonzo, 'before you ruin my party.'

Alonzo looked at her, then at the crowd. He could see that most of the kids agreed with her. 'Come on,' he said to his friends, taking Shelly's hand and starting for the door. As she went by Sal, Shelly gave him a quick look that seemed to say that she was sorry for what had happened. Alonzo stopped suddenly at the door, turned and fixed Sal with eyes flashing with anger.

'You think you're hot just because you've got that big-name agent. Well, you're not as hot as you think. Don't forget what I said, D'Angelo. I'm going to blow you away!'

9 **pop-eyed** [pɑːpʼaɪd] having eyes that are wide open – 14 **to freak out** to go mad, lose control – 17 **to spin sb around** to cause sb to turn around quickly

12 PEACE?

Monday started off badly for Sal. He slept too long and arrived at school at the last minute. Hurrying through the corridor, he noticed something white on his locker door. When he got closer, he saw that
5 it was a white feather, stuck there with a – yuck! – big piece of gum. His first thoughts were: white feather = dove = symbol of peace. But suddenly he remembered Big Zo's rap and his skin went cold. He'd called Sal a feather. A feather he was going to
10 blow away!

At lunch, Sal sat with George and Marty and showed them the feather. They talked about what it meant. Was it a joke? No, it wasn't just a joke. Was it a threat? Yeah, it was a threat. A serious threat? Yeah,
15 it was a serious threat. Should they do something about it? Yeah, but what?

In the end, they agreed that the best thing to do was for Sal to have a talk with Alonzo. George and Marty said they would tell Alonzo to meet Sal the
20 next day behind the gym at the beginning of Lunch Break – alone.

The rest of the day Sal's mind was in hyper-drive, thinking about that meeting.

---

3 **corridor** [ˈkɔːrədɚ] a long passage in a building – 20 **gym** [dʒɪm] short for gymnasium: the place where people do indoor sports

13 HEAVY TALK

As Sal waited, he grew more nervous by the minute. What if Alonzo didn't come alone? What if three or four of his crew were with him? George had said that he and Marty could hide and watch just in
5 case, but Sal had told them he could trust Alonzo.

Now he wasn't so sure.

Just then Alonzo came around the corner. Alone. As he came closer, his eyes were scanning the bushes behind Sal. He doesn't trust me, either,
10 thought Sal.

Sal considered giving him a fist bump, but held back when Alonzo put his hands in his pockets and leaned against the gym wall.

'What's up, dude?'
15 Sal put his hands in his pockets, too, and leaned on the wall beside him. 'You stuck a feather on my locker, didn't you?'

'Maybe.'

Sal forced a smile. 'It doesn't have to be like this,
20 you know.'

'Like what?' Alonzo said in a bored tone of voice.

'You know what I mean. You against me.'

'I don't know what you're talking about, man.'

Sal shook his head. 'You and I have a lot in
25 common. We – '

'Come on, D'Angelo. Not that again!'

'We're both rappers. We both love fitting words to a beat.'

Alonzo shook his head. 'That may be true, but like
30 I told you before, there's one thing we don't have in

3 **crew** [kruː] clique, group – 11 **fist bump** To show that they are friends, two people hit their tightly closed hands together

49

common: the crap you rap about don't belong to rap. No way.'

'I got it. The ghetto. Street violence, drug dealing, easy women – *that's* what rap's about.' There was an ironic smile on Sal's face.

'That's it. That's real life, the way life is in the ghetto,' Alonzo said, his voice growing loud. 'And it's what non-ghetto young people identify with. Who gives a shit about middle-class life with its ridiculous problems like a girl who freaks out cause her college blew her off?'

For a long moment, Sal only stared at Alonzo. Finally, he said, 'What's going on here? Why are you so wired about the middle class? It's your life. It's your roots, too. Could it be that you're running from something? Hiding something?'

'Hey, who do you think you are? A part-time social worker? Are you expecting me to tell you some sad story about my life? Well, you're not going to get one.' Alonzo shook his head. For the next few moments he said nothing. Then suddenly, a twisted smile crossed his face.

'Listen, man! I'm gonna tell you the facts of life. Rap is a huge industry. And the reason it got that way is because rappers are into things young guys can identify with.'

'I get it. Rap's a business and as a business it's out to give people what they want. What sells! Like lots of violence and sex and stuff like that!'

Alonzo let out a nervous laugh.

'You don't expect rappers to be better than everyone else, do you? Better than the brothers and sisters they grow up with?'

---

4 **easy women** women who readily have sex – 9 **to give a shit** *(vulg, sl)* to care –
10 **cause** [kɔz] *(abb, sl)* because – 11 **to blow sb off** *(inf)* to ignore someone's wishes –
15 **roots** the place or culture you and your family grew up in, which you have now left –
27 **to be out to** to be trying to get or do sth

He shook his head.

'No, no, rappers say it like it is. Like I said, they're into real life – reality, man. Like, they're reporters, not preachers!'

Just then a boy and girl, holding hands, came around the corner. When they saw Sal and Alonzo, they turned and disappeared around the corner again.

Sal tried to look Alonzo in the eye, but he continued to look off into the distance.

'You say rappers are reporters but what they report is more like a cartoon than real life. Their raps are full of the stereotyped ideas people have of ghetto life, things people *want* to believe about the ghetto. And the sad thing is, people *do* believe what they say.'

For the first time, Alonzo turned to face Sal. He was trying to appear cool but Sal could see the anger in his eyes.

'What about when you rapped about the twit who lost her college? Were you more than a reporter? No, man. You were showing middle-class life like it is. Hyped-up kids stressed out about college. That's what middle-class life is like – shit like that!'

For a moment Sal scanned Alonzo's face. He hesitated. Finally, he said, 'I know about your father.'

'What?'

'That he left you and your mom for another woman, a white woman. How old were you then? Nine? Ten?'

Alonzo looked away.

---

2 **to say it like it is** to tell the truth – 4 **preacher** ['priːtʃə·] a person who gives religious talks to people in church – 23 **hyped-up** [ˌhaɪpt'ʌp] excited

'It's none of my business but you must be angry at him – and her, aren't you?'

Alonzo's head snapped around. 'You're goddamned right. It *is* none of your goddamned
5 business, dude!'

'Okay, okay, I didn't mean to offend you.' Sal raised his hands to show that he had gone too far. Alonzo's face was dark with rage.

'Just keep your nose out of my business from now
10 on. Otherwise you'll be sorry!'

'Right,' Sal said, nodding his head.

For what felt to Sal like several minutes, Alonzo didn't say another word. Then, suddenly:

'You're planning to be at the Frisco Freestyle Final
15 next week, I heard.'

'I am.'

'Maybe you'd better change your plans. If you come up against me, I'll diss you so bad you'll never want to rap again!' Alonzo gave a loud laugh,
20 turned and walked away.

Sal watched him go. We'll see about that, he said to himself.

---

3 **to snap around** to turn quickly – 4 **goddamned** ['gɑːdæmd] *(off)* This word is a swear word which has no meaning. It is an expression of Alonzo's anger. – 6 **to offend** to make sb feel bad because of sth you say or do that is unfriendly – 8 **rage** [reɪdʒ] extreme anger – 14 **freestyle** ['friːstaɪl] *here:* a form of rapping in which the words are improvised during the rap battle

14 FOR SHELLY

There was a huge crowd at the Frisco Freestyle Final, larger by far than any crowd Sal had ever performed for. He had won his first two battles and was standing at the back of the stage, waiting
5 for his third, looking around at the crowd. Marty and George were on the side, near the front. They gave him the thumbs-up sign and he smiled at them. Suddenly, his eye fell on one of Alonzo's crew, pushing his way into the front row. Then he saw the
10 others, coming behind him, pushing and shoving. Of course, it was the place to be, the place nearest the action – and the judges! Right up close like that, they just might be able to influence the judges to vote for their man. One look in those angry faces,
15 Sal thought, could influence any judge.

Sal's first reaction was red-hot anger. He turned to glare at Alonzo, but he was over in the shadows, doing push-ups, getting pumped up for his next performance. For a moment, Sal thought of
20 confronting Alonzo with this, but quickly realized that that would be a dumb move. The smart thing to do was to calm down and get ready for his next performance. Telling himself to ignore Alonzo and his crew, he closed his eyes and forced himself to
25 concentrate.

When it was his turn again, he was ready and he gave another strong performance. While looking around and waiting for the judges to announce who won, Sal suddenly noticed Shelly, standing in

---

7 **thumbs-up** [ˌθʌmz'ʌp] A sign made by sticking up your thumb to show you like, agree with or support sb / sth – 10 **to shove** [ʃʌv] to push sb / sth in a rough way – 18 **push-ups** an exercise in which you lie face down and raise your body off the ground by pushing down with your hands until your arms are straight – 18 **to get pumped up** to get physically and mentally ready

the front row, trying to catch his eye. The look on her face made him take a sharp breath. It seemed to say, I'm pulling for you, I want *you* to win!

A moment later, she smiled and the crowd applauded wildly when the judges named him the winner.

At the end of the evening, there were only two rappers left: Sal D and Big Zo. The crowd buzzed with excitement when the MC announced that the final battle was about to begin. There would be three one-minute rounds, he said, handing Big Zo the microphone. Big Zo gave his crew a knowing smile, then pushed his face into Sal's and began.

> *This is Sal D*
> *from Albany,*
> *where the grass is greener,*
> *the people cleaner*
> *than Mr. Clean.*
> *He's as proud as can be*
> *of Albany.*
> *That's okay,*
> *if only he'd stay there.*
> *But no!*
> *He won't stay home,*
> *he gotta get into*
> *the San Francisco rap scene,*
> *thinks there's room for him,*
> *don't know that he's*
> *a fish out of water,*
> *a fish in the wrong water.*
> *This is deep water,*
> *dark water,*

---

9 **MC** Master of Ceremonies (the person who introduces the rappers and entertains the audience)

shark water,
no-place-for-little-fish-after-dark-water.
This ain't no swimming pool,
didn't yo momma tell you,
5 *it's the ocean, man.*
You're in the ocean now,
unnerstand?
Where the BIG FISH play,
it's way over your head, man,
10 *you're dead, man,*
you can't survive,
BIG FISH gonna eat you alive!

Finishing, Big Zo opened his mouth wide as if he was about to take a bite out of Sal. The crowd
15 loved his performance and gave him a long and enthusiastic round of applause. Sal took a deep breath. He realized that he was in for the hardest battle of the night. He had known that Alonzo would diss him about Albany, but hadn't expected
20 him to do such a good job of it!

In his answer Sal emphasized that yes, he *was* proud of his hometown. But, he explained, anyone who listened carefully to his raps knew that it wasn't blind pride. His love for Albany was a tough love,
25 about the dark side of life there, the side the people of the town preferred to ignore. He also emphasized that the 'ocean' is a big place with room for all kinds of 'fish' and that smaller ones were sometimes better at surviving than the larger kind. When he
30 finished, there was lots of loud applause. Still, Sal wasn't sure who had won the first round. The judges didn't seem to be sure, either. Alonzo, on the other

---

7 **unnerstand** understand – 11 **to survive** [səˈvaɪv] to continue to live or exist –
24 **blind pride** to feel good about sth without knowing why

hand, was looking around at the crowd with a big winner's grin on his face.

Knowing he would go first in the next round, Sal thought fast, scanning his brain for a good idea to
5 start with. Before he knew it, the new beat started up and the MC handed him the mike. It's diss time, Sal said to himself. He closed his eyes a moment and concentrated on the beat. He began with the well-known saying, 'Beware of wolves in sheep's
10 clothing', but turned it upside down!

> *Who's afraid of the big bad wolf?*
> *Who's afraid of Big Zo?*
> *Wants you to think he's a big bad wolf,*
> *but no!*
15 *He's just a sheep in wolves' clothing,*
> *with his cornrows*
> *and hip-hop clothes,*
> *tattoos,*
> *ring in his nose.*
20 *He wants you to think*
> *he's from the ghetto,*
> *but it's a fake ID!*
> *He's no wolf,*
> *he's a sheep,*
25 *a black sheep,*
> *A middle-class black sheep*
> *from Albany.*

It was a strong performance and the crowd was laughing all the way through.
30 When he finished, Sal took a good look at Alonzo. Surprisingly, he still had that winner's grin on his

---

9 **to beware of** to be careful of – 15 **sheep in wolves' clothing** He is less dangerous than he looks. – 16 **cornrows** ['kɔːrnrouz] a hair style in which the hair is twisted in straight lines close to the head

face. The MC waited a moment while the crowd quieted down, then gave him the microphone. He looked Sal in the eye, poked his finger at him and started.

5   *Be careful of Sal D,*
       seems so friendly.
       See his smile?
       You think: sweet guy,
       wouldn't hurt a fly,
10   *I wanna take him home with me.*
       But that smile is a lie
       he hides behind,
       a net he fishes with,
       pulls in his fishes with,
15   *guys like you an' me,*
       get pulled in
       and cut to pieces
       on the sharp edges
       of his irony.

20 This was good stuff and the crowd ate it up. When the rap was over, Sal felt his heart beat faster. Alonzo had surprised him again. He was pumped up and performing brilliantly.

Who won the round? Sal didn't know, but of
25 one thing he was sure: if he was going to win the battle, he would have to be at his best the last time around. He stood back and waited, knowing that it was Alonzo's turn to go first and wondering what he'd say this time. As he waited, he turned his eyes
30 towards Shelly. She was looking at him and nodding as though saying, come on, Sal, you can do it! A

---

19 **irony** [ˈaɪrəni] the use of words that say the opposite of what you mean, e.g. you say 'You're so friendly to me' when you mean that the person is not at all friendly to you.

warm smile, starting down deep inside, crossed Sal's face and he nodded back: yes, I can. This one's for you!

His thoughts came to a sudden end when he felt
5 a finger pushing into his chest. It was Alonzo's! The final round had begun!

> This is Sal D,
> D for duh?
> Don't know diddly-squat
> 10 about rap, nada, man.
> He gonna try to diss me,
> piss me,
> hiss his flag
> on the high ground
> 15 and say hey!
> This is my ground.
> He laughs at me
> 'cause of my jewelry,
> makes fun of my clunkers,
> 20 claims I'm a clunker-junkie,
> says I shine on the outside
> but I'm all dark inside.
> Sure, I like the shine
> of gold and silver.
> 25 Does that make him any better?
> Is it a crime
> to wear a gold chain,
> a sin
> to love rings and things?
> 30 Sal D
> don't have a clue
> about dressing fine,

---

8 **duh** *(inf) here:* a stupid person – 9 **diddly-squat** [ˌdɪdliˈskwɑːt] *(inf)* nothing – 10 **nada** *(Spanish)* nothing – 18 **jewelry** [ˈdʒuːəlri] objects such as rings and necklaces that people wear as decoration – 19 **clunker** *(inf)* piece of jewelry – 28 **sin** very bad behavior

runs around in T-shirt and jeans
all the time,
thinking fashion means
looking ordinary,
5 *blending in like a million*
other chameleons,
so no one's gonna notice him.
He takes understatement
to a new low level.
10 *He's so understated*
he's invisible,
I mean you walk by him
and don't see him.
Just another nerd in T-shirt and jeans,
15 *a sheep in a herd of sheep,*
don't appear on your radar screen.
Look at his clothes!
What do they say?
Don't pay
20 *no attention to me,*
feel sorry for me,
I got no personality!

The crowd went wild. Their applause was long and loud, especially from the front row. Again, 25 Sal was taken by surprise. Alonzo had saved his best performance for last. He had used the same strategy as in the first round: taking away Sal's chance to diss on something important by talking about it before. That was clever! He had taken up 30 Sal's diss on his jewelry – the one Sal had used so effectively at Alicia's party – so Sal couldn't repeat it. And he had dissed Sal for the way he dressed!

---

5 **to blend in** Sth blends in when it is so similar to the background that it is difficult to see it separately. – 14 **nerd** [nɜːrd] *(sl)* a person who is boring, stupid and not fashionable

Sal was under pressure now. He took a quick look at Shelly, then closed his eyes, listened for the beat, and came out fighting.

Big Zo
5   *dissin' my clothes*
is like a Chevy
dissin' a Rolls,
but I won't go into that,
I'll leave it to you to know
10   *who don't know nothin'*
about clothes.
Let's talk about his walk,
like a cock in the chicken pen,
like John Wayne in a Western
15   *or W on the deck of the carrier.*
His walk seems to say
'Out of my way!
I'm coming like it or not.'
His walk is bad,
20   *but when he opens his mouth*
things get worse.
His rap is fantasy,
straight from the dictionary
of slang, man,
25   *has to look it up, man.*
His rap is plastic,
a product of research,
don't come from the heart.
Only a dude who's
30   *never been in the ghetto*
sounds like that.

---

6 **Chevy** [ˈʃəvi] short for "Chevrolet", an American automobile brand, often seen as ordinary and nothing special (the opposite of a Rolls Royce) – 7 **Rolls** Rolls Royce, a very exclusive British car brand – 13 **cock** an adult male chicken – 15 **W on the deck of the carrier** George W. Bush on the ship in 2003 saying that the war in Iraq was over

And that's the biggest joke of all,
he goin' on and on about the ghetto
as if he knows what he's talkin' about.
As if it's from his soul.
5 *All the knowledge he got*
about the ghetto
he took from other rappers,
he hooked it.
His rap is patchwork,
10 *a little bit of 50 Cent,*
a line or two from Coolio,
something from Snoop Dogg
and Eminem.
From Nelly
15 *and Missy Elliott*
he also hooks.
He's a rat, a pi – rat,
the Johnny Depp
of the rapper scene
20 *without the good looks!*

Sal's strong ending went down well with the crowd. They were laughing and applauding at the same time. Sal looked around to see how the judges were reacting, but they had moved to the back of the 25 stage already, their heads close together. Little by little, the crowd quieted down. Soon, everyone was staring at the judges, waiting for their decision.

---

8 **to hook** *(inf)* to take sth that doesn't belong to you – 17 **pi – rat** [ˈpaɪˌræt] pirate –
21 **to go down well with** to be liked by

15 THE WINNER

Several minutes went by. The crowd grew even quieter. Sal glanced at Alonzo. He was standing at the front of the stage, smiling down at his crew. He looked very sure of himself. Sal looked at Shelly but
5 she looked away.

Finally, the judges ended their discussion and came to the front. One of them, an older man with long gray hair, was given the microphone. 'It wasn't easy for us to decide on a winner tonight,' he
10 began in a nervous voice. 'I think you'll agree that this final was one of the best freestyle battles seen here in years. Both of the rappers gave brilliant performances, both deserved to win. Unfortunately, the rules say there can be only one winner.'

15 Suddenly, Alonzo's crew began chanting, 'Big Zo, Big Zo, Big Zo!' Alonzo smiled and waved his arms in the air, motioning for the crowd to join in. Shaken, the judge with the microphone took a quick step back. Sal saw red. This was really unfair.

20 After a while, the judge with the microphone raised his arm for silence. The chant continued for a moment, then faded. 'After a long discussion,' he began again, his voice even shakier than before, 'we are ready to announce our decision. The winner
25 is... Big Zo!'

The words no sooner left his mouth than the crowd began to boo. The judges motioned for them to calm down, but the booing only grew louder. The judges looked at each other, helplessly.

---

13 **to deserve** [dɪˈzɜːv] If sb deserves sth, it is right that they should have it. – 19 **to see red** to become angry – 22 **to fade** [feɪd] to become quieter

Suddenly, Alonzo freaked out, grabbed the microphone and began shouting angrily at the crowd. The crowd stopped booing a moment to listen to what he was saying, then started booing
5 again, louder than before. Alonzo's face grew red with rage. Suddenly, he reached down and pulled Shelly up onto the stage beside him. He threw the microphone at the crowd, turned with Shelly and started for the back exit. They had only taken a few
10 steps when Shelly cried out and tried to pull away from him. Alonzo held onto her and dragged her towards the exit. Shocked, Sal ran to help her. At the same moment, Alonzo turned and motioned to his crew to follow him. They ran onto the stage and
15 were just about to grab Sal when George and Marty came at them from behind. A wild fight started.

Almost immediately, several huge security men stormed onto the stage and began to pull the boys apart. It took them several minutes to stop the fight.
20 Alonzo was kicking and shouting as they took him and his crew away.

Sal looked around for Shelly and called out her name. Crying softly, she came out of the shadows at the back of the stage, where she had hidden during
25 the fight. When Sal saw her frightened face, he nodded and held out his arms to her. Shelly moved toward him hesitantly. Suddenly, she looked behind her, as if expecting Alonzo to come out of the darkness to take her with him. But there, between
30 her and the darkness, stood Marty and George, tall and strong and smiling at her. Slowly, she turned back to Sal, then hurried into his waiting arms. When she raised her head, Sal's lips were waiting, too. It was a long, warm kiss.

11 **to drag** to pull along with difficulty – 18 **to storm** to come quickly and noisily – 20 **to kick** to move your legs as if you were hitting sth

Tasks and Projects

Before reading

1. Make a list of five or six famous American rappers, including the name of at least one of their hits.

2. Watch some videos of rap battles on the Internet. Write down your first impressions and be ready to share them with the class. For example:

   What do the rappers rap about?

   Do you like rap music? Why (not)?

   Can you find different sorts of rap music? What are the differences?

While reading

Chapter by chapter, answer these questions or do the tasks.

Chapter One

1. In pairs or small groups, do some research on the town of Albany (California) on the Internet. Make a list of interesting facts about Albany.

2. In small groups, discuss what Alonzo thinks of Sal rapping about middle-class life.

   Report your opinion(s) to the class.

Chapter Two

Do some research on the Internet and find some examples of the connection between the rap scene in America and violence.

Chapter Three

1. Using Sal's outside-inside technique, write a short rap about someone you know or someone famous.

2. Summarize what the rap says about Marie in a few sentences.

Chapter Four

1. In pairs, choose any 30 lines from the chapter, pick a role and perform the dialogue, reading only what the characters say.

2. In small groups, discuss the way Shelly relates to Alonzo. Share your opinion(s) with the class.

Chapter Five

1. Taking turns, the whole class reads the dialogue (only what is said) between Alonzo and Sal, beginning where Sal says, 'Wait a minute. I want to talk to you.'

2. In pairs, talk about Sal's way of thinking about rapping. Be prepared to report your thoughts to the class.

Chapter Six

1. Chapter Six can be divided into several mini-scenes, e.g. what happens at Minna's.

   In small groups, choose one scene and prepare to mime it (no words!) for the class.

2. In pairs, imagine a short conversation between Sal and his mother after she has met Marty and George. Be ready to perform your dialogue for the class.

Chapter Seven

1. In pairs, choose one of the two scenes in the chapter (Sal at Mr. Silverton's / Sal at home) and prepare to perform it in class.

2. In small groups, talk about what you think of Sal's mother signing the contract. Why did she sign it? Do you think she was right to sign it? Be prepared to report your opinion(s) to the class.

Chapter Eight

1. Taking turns, the whole class performs the dialogue between Sal and his mother, beginning where his mother says, 'Hi, Sal.' (page 34, line 12).

2. In pairs, discuss situations in which you or people you know have 'crossed the line'. Be ready to share your thoughts about this with the class.

Chapter Nine

In pairs, choose a role and practice the little scene in which Shelly stops and talks with Sal. Be ready to perform the scene.

Chapter Ten

1. There are several short scenes in Chapter Ten, e.g. Alicia welcoming Sal to her party. In small groups, choose one of these scenes and get ready to perform it for the class.

2. In pairs, try to imagine what:

   a) Sal is thinking when he says to Alicia, 'Bring him on!'

   b) Alicia thinks when she hears Sal say this.

   Formulate your ideas and share them with the class.

Chapter Eleven

1. In groups, prepare to perform Sal's rap about Big Zo ('Big Zo is a hot shot...').

2. In groups of four, choose roles (Sal, Big Zo, Alicia, George) and get ready to perform the final scene of the chapter, beginning when the applause for Sal's rap died down (page 47, line 6).

Chapter Twelve

In groups of three, think up some dialogue for the scene at lunch, when Sal talks with George and Marty about the feather. Prepare to perform the scene for the class.

Chapter Thirteen

1. Two pairs of pupils are chosen. After a few moments for preparation, the first pair performs the dialogue (only what is said), then the second pair does the same. (Begin with 'What's up, dude?'). (page 49, line 14)

   In small groups, the others in the class discuss the performances and offer comments.

2. In pairs, think about and comment on one or more of Alonzo's ideas about rapping.

Chapter Fourteen

The best rappers in the class are divided into two teams, the Sal team and the Alonzo team. Each team gets ready to perform the raps in the same order as in the story:

FIRST ROUND   – Big Zo: 'This is Sal D from Albany...' (pages 54 and 55)

SECOND ROUND   – Sal: 'Who's afraid of the big bad wolf?' (page 56, lines 11 to 27)
                 – Big Zo: 'Be careful of Sal D...' (page 57, lines 5 to 19)

FINAL ROUND   – Big Zo: 'This is Sal D, D for duh?' (pages 58 and 59)
– Sal: 'Big Zo dissin' my clothes...' (pages 60 and 61)

In small groups, the rest of the class play the role of the judges. They discuss the performances. One of the 'judges' from each group then gives a little speech announcing the winner, giving reasons for the group's decision.

After reading

1. In groups, choose a scene from any part of the story and make a video film or a photo story of it. (You should be able to find free download software on the Internet which enables you to put together digital images with text, music and narration in the form of a photo-movie.)

2. If the class's performance of the rap battle turned out well (Chapter 14), it might be fun to perform it for different audiences, such as another class or several classes.

Project: A Poll: How Popular is Rap Music?

A good way to find out what pupils think about rap music is to take a poll.

Using the table on the next page, ask at least five students from other classes about their favorite (rap) music:

How Popular is Rap Music?

	Student 1	Student 2	Student 3	Student 4	Student 5
What kinds of music do you like?					
Why do you like rap music?					
Why don't you like rap music?					
Who are your favorite rappers?					
What are your favorite rap songs?					

Write a summary of your findings.

AND / OR

Present the results of your poll to the class.